I0201600

EMOTIONS and FEELINGS

Gratitude

Kari Jones

Explore other books at:
WWW.ENGAGEBOOKS.COM

VANCOUVER, B.C.

WWW.ENGAGEBOOKS.COM

Gratitude: Level 2
Emotions and Feelings
Jones, Kari 1966 –
Text © 2023 Engage Books
Design © 2023 Engage Books

Edited by: A.R. Roumanis, Ashley Lee,
Melody Sun, and Sarah Harvey
Design by: Mandy Christiansen

Text set in Arial Regular.
Chapter headings set in PeachyKeenJF.

FIRST EDITION / FIRST PRINTING

All rights reserved. No part of this book may be stored in a retrieval system, reproduced or transmitted in any form or by any other means without written permission from the publisher or a licence from the Canadian Copyright Licensing Agency. Critics and reviewers may quote brief passages in connection with a review or critical article in any media.

Every reasonable effort has been made to contact the copyright holders of all material reproduced in this book.

LIBRARY AND ARCHIVES CANADA CATALOGUING IN PUBLICATION

Title: Gratitude / Kari Jones.
Names: Jones, Kari (Kari Lynne), 1966- author.
Description: Series statement: Emotions and feelings

Identifiers: Canadiana (print) 20230134971 | Canadiana (ebook) 20230134998
ISBN 978-1-77878-145-2 (hardcover)
ISBN 978-1-77878-146-9 (softcover)
ISBN 978-1-77878-147-6 (epub)
ISBN 978-1-77878-148-3 (pdf)
ISBN 978-1-77878-149-0 (audio)

Subjects:
LCSH: Gratitude—Juvenile literature.
LCSH: Gratitude in children—Juvenile literature.

Classification: LCC BF723.S87 J66 2023 | DDC J152.4—DC23

This project has been made possible in part by the Government of Canada.

Canada

Contents

4 What Is Gratitude?

6 Why Do People Feel Grateful?

8 Are There Different Kinds of Gratitude?

10 How Does Gratitude Affect the Way You Think?

12 How Does Gratitude Affect the Way You Act?

14 Is Gratitude Always a Good Thing?

16 Does Everyone Feel Grateful?

18 What Does Gratitude Feel Like?

20 Can You Make Yourself Feel Grateful?

22 Does Gratitude Ever Go Away?

24 Does Gratitude Change as You Grow Older?

26 What Can You Do if You Do Not Feel Grateful?

28 How Can You Help Other People Feel Grateful?

30 Quiz

What Is Gratitude?

Gratitude is a **positive** emotion. It is the feeling of being thankful. Someone who feels gratitude is grateful. You can be grateful for things like a home, friends, and family.

KEY WORD

Positive: good or useful.

Gratitude means taking time to **value** the good things in your life. It helps make people happy. Clean drinking water and parks to play in are things people can be grateful for.

KEY WORD

Value: understand the importance of something.

Why Do People Feel Gratitude?

People feel grateful when good things happen. They may be grateful for different things at different times.

You can be grateful for something that does not happen. If your tooth hurts, you might be scared to go to the dentist. You may be grateful when you find out it does not need to be pulled.

People often feel grateful when someone is kind to them.

Are There Different Kinds of Gratitude?

There are three kinds of gratitude. It can be a mood that comes and goes throughout the day. It can also be a **temporary** feeling you get when something good happens to you.

KEY WORD

Temporary: lasting for only a short period of time.

Gratitude can also be a way of living your life. People who live with gratitude try to be thankful for everything they have even when it is difficult.

How Does Gratitude Affect the Way You Think?

Gratitude helps us enjoy what is going on right now. Grateful people value things. You will value a new toy longer if you are grateful for it.

Girls and women often say they feel grateful more often than boys and men.

Gratitude blocks **negative** emotions. It is not possible to be grateful and angry at the same time.

KEY WORD

Negative: not pleasant or not helpful.

How Does Gratitude Affect the Way You Act?

Gratitude makes us more **resilient**. Grateful people understand that life has ups and downs. They are able to feel better faster after something bad happens.

KEY WORD

Resilient: able to recover from hard things quickly.

Gratitude leads to action. Grateful people are **generous** and happy. You will likely share your toys if you are grateful for your friend.

KEY WORD

Generous: giving more than is expected.

Is Gratitude Always a Good Thing?

If you are told to be grateful, you may not feel real gratitude. Real gratitude is always given by choice.

Faking gratitude can make you feel angry or sad. No one should try to make you feel grateful.

Does Everyone Feel Grateful?

Anyone can feel grateful. But some people have a harder time feeling grateful. Some people feel grateful more often than others.

You can be grateful for small things like new shoes or big things like feeling safe.

People who feel **entitled** are less likely to be grateful. Ungrateful people are often less happy. They often have a hard time connecting with others.

KEY WORD

Entitled: when someone feels they should get everything they want.

17

What Does Gratitude Feel Like?

Gratitude can make your body feel calm. Your breath might slow down. You might even feel warm.

Stress: when people feel uncomfortable about something that is happening.

Gratitude is good for your mental health. It reduces **stress**. This can make you feel happier.

19

Can You Make Yourself Feel Grateful?

You cannot make yourself feel grateful for something you are not actually thankful for. But you can learn to live your life with more gratitude.

Living your life with gratitude takes practice. You have to look for things to be grateful for with purpose.

Does Gratitude Ever Go Away?

It can be hard to hold on to gratitude. It is a **fleeting** emotion for many people. It comes and goes.

KEY WORD

Fleeting: lasting a very short time.

Sometimes gratitude can stay a long time. If you work hard to live your life with gratitude, you can feel grateful every day.

Does Gratitude Change as You Grow Older?

There are some things you may always be grateful for. Most people are always grateful for kindness and love.

24

Some things you are grateful for will change as you grow older. Children are often grateful for their toys. Adults may be grateful to have a good job.

Being grateful can help you feel hopeful.

What Can You Do if You Do Not Feel Grateful?

Take a moment to feel grateful for one thing every day. You might be grateful your mom made you breakfast.

Think about someone you are grateful for. Could you do something kind for them today?

How Can You Help Other People Feel Grateful?

Be kind to your friends and family. Tell them you are happy they are in your life. Remind people that kindness is something to be grateful for.

You cannot make people feel grateful. You can help them feel happy. They might be grateful you did.

Quiz

Test your knowledge of gratitude by answering the following questions. The questions are based on what you have read in this book. The answers are listed on the bottom of the next page.

1 How many kinds of gratitude are there?

2 What does the word "generous" mean?

3 Who are less likely to be grateful?

4 Is gratitude good for your mental health?

5 What are most people always grateful for?

6 Can you make people grateful?

Explore other books in the Emotions and Feelings series.

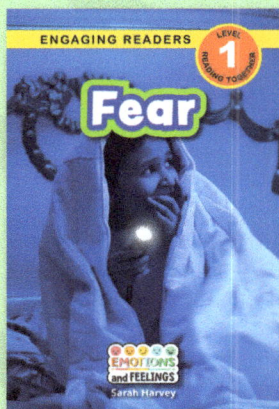

ENGAGING READERS · LEVEL 1 · READING TOGETHER — **Fear** · Sarah Harvey

ENGAGING READERS · LEVEL 1 · READING TOGETHER — **Happiness** · Karl Jones

ENGAGING READERS · LEVEL 1 · READING TOGETHER — **Sadness** · Sarah Harvey

ENGAGING READERS · LEVEL 1 · READING TOGETHER — **Surprise** · Karl Jones

ENGAGING READERS · LEVEL 2 · READING WITH HELP — **Gratitude** · Karl Jones

ENGAGING READERS · LEVEL 2 · READING WITH HELP — **Grief** · Sarah Harvey

ENGAGING READERS · LEVEL 2 · READING WITH HELP — **Guilt** · Sarah Harvey

ENGAGING READERS · LEVEL 2 · READING WITH HELP — **Love** · Sarah Harvey

ENGAGING READERS · LEVEL 2 · READING WITH HELP — **Worry** · Sarah Harvey

Visit www.engagebooks.com/readers

Answers: 1. Three 2. Giving more than is expected 3. People who feel entitled 4. Yes 5. Kindness and love 6. No

www.ingramcontent.com/pod-product-compliance
Lightning Source LLC
Chambersburg PA
CBHW051236020426
42331CB00016B/3405